W9-AAZ-769

Big Machines At Work

Concrete Mixers

By Jean Eick

The Child's World® Inc. ◆ Eden Prairie, Minnesota

Published by The Child's World®, Inc.
7081 W. 192 Ave.
Eden Prairie, MN 55346

Design and Production:
The Creative Spark, San Juan Capistrano, CA.

Photos: © 1998 David M. Budd Photography

Library of Congress Cataloging-in-Publication Data
Eick, Jean, 1947-
        Concrete mixers at work / by Jean Eick.
                p. cm.
        Includes index.
        Summary: Briefly describes the parts of a concrete mixer and how it works.
        ISBN 1-56766-527-6 (library reinforced : alk. paper)
        1. Concrete mixers--Juvenile literature. [1. Concrete mixers.] I. Title.
TA439.E33 1998
624.1'834--dc21   98-3132
                                                                  CIP
                                                                  AC

Contents

On the Job

On the job, **concrete** mixers work at building sites. Concrete is used to make sidewalks, basements, and the walls of many buildings.

Concrete is made from water, cement, sand, and small stones. As the mixture sits, it gets very hard. The concrete mixer brings the thick mixture right to where the workers need it.

7

8

The big truck goes from job to job. As it goes down the road, a big **drum** on the back turns round and round. Inside the drum, the concrete is stirred by a giant **blade**. The drum and the blade mix the concrete as they turn.

Beep, beep! The truck slowly backs up. On the back of the truck is a giant slide called a **chute**. The chute is used for pouring the concrete. The driver places the chute right where the concrete is needed.

Here comes the concrete!

Quickly, the construction workers push the concrete into place.

The big chute is put back into place

on the truck.

Now the truck is ready to go to the next

job. Round and round turns the drum!

Climb Aboard!

Would you like to see inside the truck? Climb aboard! The big mirrors help the driver see where to back up. The big wheel lets the driver turn the truck and change directions. There are also lots of buttons for the driver to push.

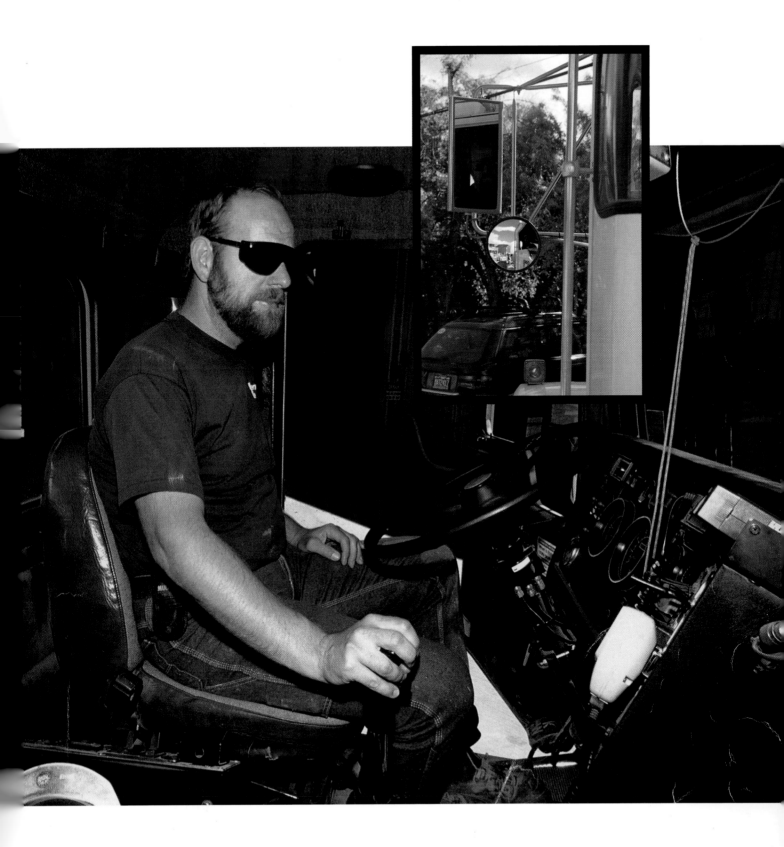

Up Close

1. The cab

2. The drum

3. The blade

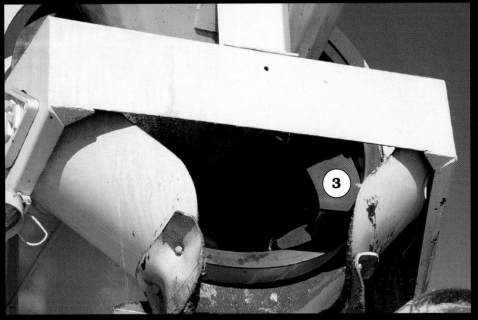

4. The chute

5. The ingredients

Glossary

blade (BLADE)
The blade is a big, flat piece of metal that mixes the concrete.

chute (SHOOT)
The chute is a slide that folds down from the back of the truck. The concrete slides down the chute.

concrete (KON-kreet)
Concrete is a mixture of water, sand, cement, and small stones. It is used for making sidewalks, basements, and walls.

drum (DRUM)
The drum is the round mixer on the back of the truck. The drum turns round and round.